A PROMISE DEFERRED

The Massacre of Black Wall Street

Written By

Dr. Tamecca S. Rogers and Keith Ross

Illustrated by **Arushan Art**

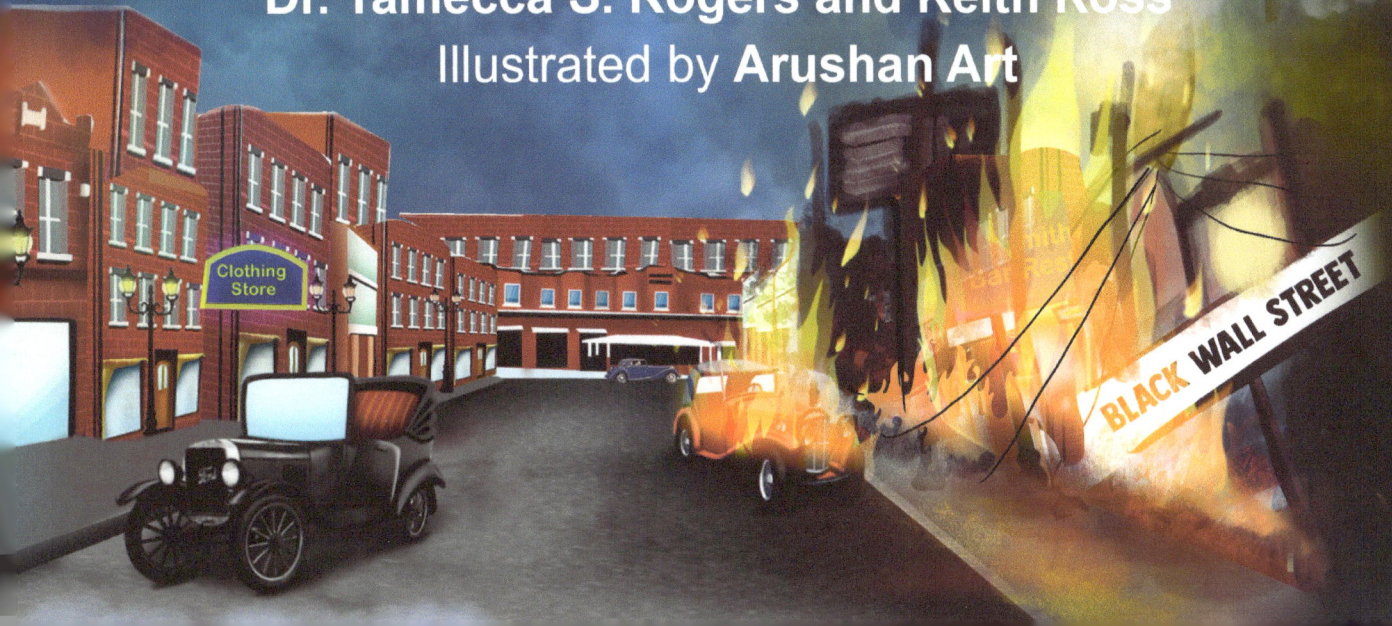

About the Authors

Dr. Tamecca Rogers holds a bachelor's degree in psychology, a master's in business administration, and a doctoral degree in educational leadership. Dr. Rogers served five years as a hospital corpsman in the United States Navy and a combined six years as a high school instructor and college enrollment counselor. She has also held adjunct professor positions at multiple postsecondary institutions. Dr. Rogers has worked at Tulsa Technology Center since 2010 and currently holds the position of the Director of Diversity, Equity, and Inclusion. She is the proud mom of Ian, Chazen, and Keith, and lives in Tulsa, Oklahoma with her family.

Keith Ross is a fourth grader who loves video games, Beyblades, road trips, modeling, and acting. Keith has his own unique style and dances to his own beat. He lives in Tulsa, Oklahoma with his family.

Keith has co-authored Now You're It: Journaling to Perseverance, Momma May I Be Me?, Daddy May I Decide?, and A Promise Deferred: The Massacre of Black Wall Street, with his mother, Dr. Rogers, and this is his fourth book.

ISBN Number: 978-1-7354301-8-8
Library of Congress Control Number: 2021900112

Published by Inspire Publishing LLC
P.O. Box 691608
Tulsa, OK 74169-1608, USA

Inspire Publishing LLC

Dedication

This book is dedicated to the 1921 Tulsa Race Massacre victims and the three survivors still alive today, Hughes Van Ellis, Viola Fletcher, and Mother Lessie Benningfield Randle. A portion of proceeds from the sales of this book will be donated to the Justice for Greenwood Foundation.

"Hey, Keith, please pack your bags to go over to your grandma's house for the weekend," Keith's mom said.

"Yayyyyy! Thanks, Mom. I love spending time with my grandme. I can't wait to see her," Keith said in excitement.

"Keith, I'm so glad you came to spend time with me! What are we going to do this weekend?" Grandme asked with curiosity.

"Well, Grandme, I'm so glad you asked! I brought my video game system, and I can't wait to play with you. I brought an extra controller and everything. Do you have fast Wi-Fi? We really need fast Wi-Fi!" Keith explained.

"Video games, controllers, and fast Wi-Fi? Geez," Grandme exclaimed, "what have I got myself into this weekend? How about we have story time, instead of playing video games?"

With a puzzled look on his face, Keith asked, "Story time, Grandme?"

Grandme responded, "Yes, story time, Keith! Do you know anything about Black Wall Street?"

"Black Wall Street? No, ma'am. I've never heard of it. What's that?" Keith asked.

With a pleased look on her face, Grandme said, "OK, let's take a stroll down memory lane to the year 1921. I want to tell you a true, inspiring story of a brilliant Black business district, right here in Tulsa, Oklahoma. This is where African Americans created an economic miracle which ultimately resulted in the establishment of over 600 businesses, including a mega-church, public schools, libraries, and a hospital!"

Keith beamed with excitement and said, "Wow, Grandme! Black people created all of that in 1921? Is this true or make believe?"

Grandme excitedly replied, "Grandson, every bit is true! There were even entrepreneurial African Americans who owned hotels, theaters, clothing stores, restaurants, printing firms, transportation companies, and newspapers."

"Wow, they sound like they were busy, but what's an entrepreneur?" Keith questioned, clearly intrigued.

Grandme explained, "An entrepreneur is a person who creates their own business and provides opportunities for others. They are their own boss."

Keith was so excited and said, "Grandme, I would love to have my own business and be the boss! Was there anything fun to do on Black Wall Street?"

Grandme said with pride, "Oh, Keith, let me tell you! Black Wall Street had ice cream and candy stores, and a few dancing clubs with live entertainment, including blues and jazz music!

As a matter of fact, James, Vasinora, and Henry Nails were the first owners of Lacy Park, which included the Nails Dance Pavilion and a skating rink. They also owned a record store, which is a place where you could go to buy music. They were notable entrepreneurs who not only owned entertainment establishments, but a shoe shop and a taxi and limousine service."

"But I'm getting ahead of myself," said Grandme. "Let's start from the beginning. African Americans first traveled to Oklahoma from Texas, Arkansas, Mississippi, and Louisiana in hope of a better life. They thought they'd have a better chance to earn a living in Oklahoma, free from violence and discrimination. The Cherokee, Chickasaw, Choctaw, Creek, and Seminole Native American nations brought other African Americans here as slaves during the 1838 Trail of Tears."

"Wait a minute, Grandme, I know about the Trail of Tears, but I didn't know Black people were on that trail, and I sure did not know Native Americans owned Black slaves. Is this a joke?" Keith asked, with a disgusted look on his face.

"Oh, grandson, I wish it weren't true, but unfortunately it is," Grandme said sadly. "One third of the people who traveled on the Trail of Tears were Black slaves the Native Americans owned. After the Civil War, slaves were free in law, however, it was slow to transpire. In the 1900s, there were 27 all-Black towns in Oklahoma. However, some say it was over 60! Most Black Oklahomans moved to Tulsa in search of better opportunities. It was rumored Tulsa was the 'promised land.'"

"Grandme, why was Tulsa considered the promised land?" Keith questioned.

"Good question," Grandme replied. "Famous Oklahoma businessman John Williams called Tulsa the promised land because of the oil and wealth in the area. However, everything was still segregated like the rest of the country. Blacks and Whites had their place, and it wasn't together.

You could say the promise of the promised land was deferred. Many would argue, it still is."

REST ROOMS
WHITE   COLORED
L&N

"Grandme, what does segregated mean?" Keith asked.

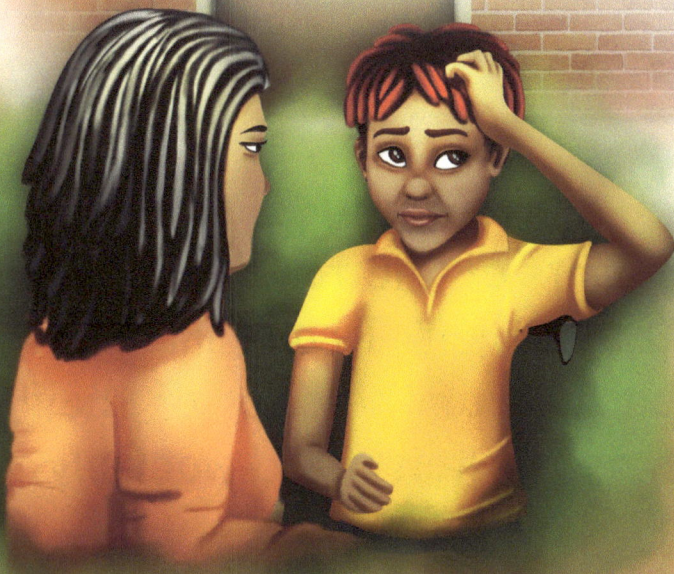

Grandme explained, "Segregation happens when a society or a country views one race as better than another, and they establish laws that separate the races.

For example, Black kids could not always attend the same schools as White kids. Tulsa was no different. Instead of one united city, some people believed the evolution of Tulsa to be the tale of two segregated cities. The White residents referred to any land north of the Frisco railroad tracks as 'Little Africa.' Greenwood Avenue, in the Black area, was important because it was one of the few streets that did not pass through both the Black and White areas. It was a solely Black area and became the center of all activity."

"Wait a minute, Grandme! Are you saying Black and White people lived in separate parts of the town, and they did not play, work, or shop together? I can't imagine not playing with my friends because of the color of their skin! That would make me sad," Keith said woefully.

"Yes, grandson, that's exactly what I am saying," answered Grandme. "Although they lived in separate parts of the town, Black residents took pride in their area because it was something they controlled. Greenwood Avenue, part of Greenwood District, grew into a commercial district of red brick buildings, thanks to the local Acme Brick Company."

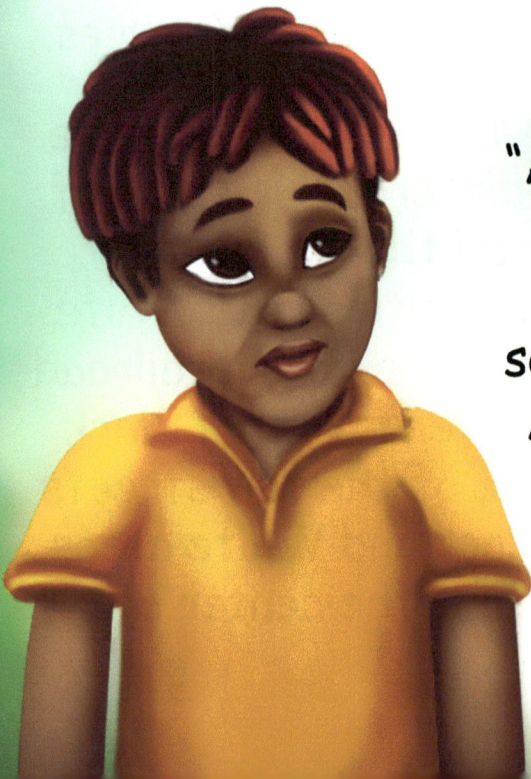

"Whoa, Grandme! What businesses were in the brick buildings of the Greenwood District?" Keith asked.

"Grandson, here comes the exciting part!" exclaimed Grandme.

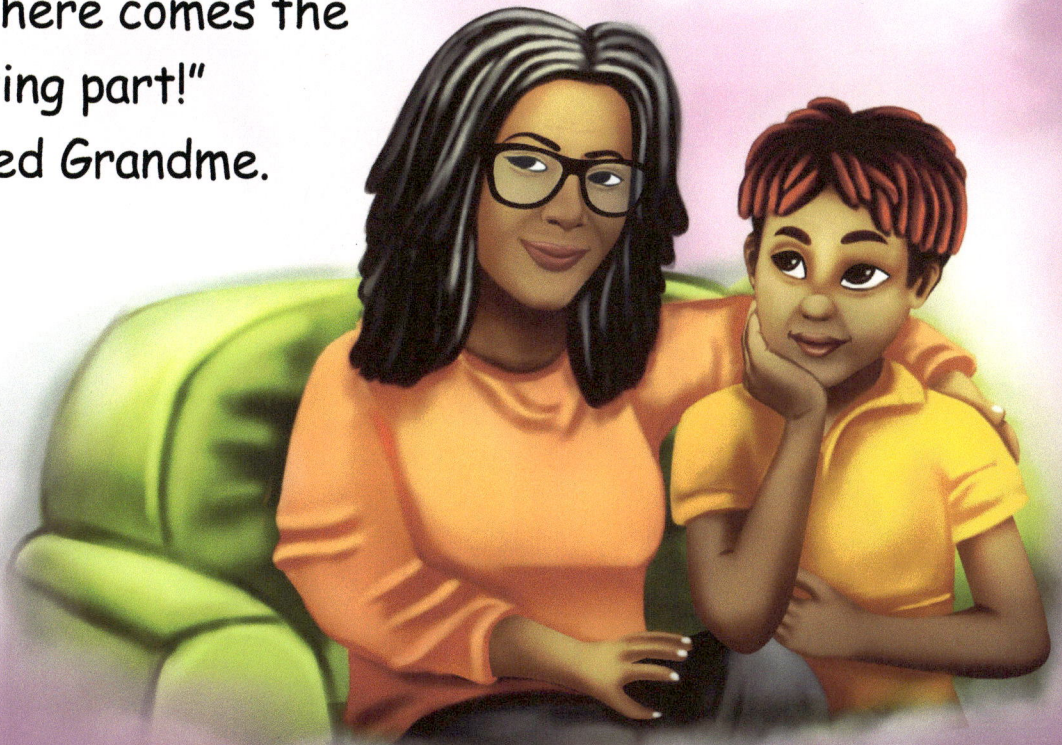

"John Williams and his wife, Loula Williams, owned a three-story building full of various businesses at 101 North Greenwood Avenue. On the ground floor, Loula Williams owned the candy store that sold candy, ice cream, and soda with room for 50 happy customers to enjoy the 12-foot water fountain! The living space for the Williams family was on the first floor. On the second floor, attorneys, doctors, and a dentist rented office space for their practices," Grandme said.

"Wow, Grandme! How exciting to have all that in one building," Keith said.

"Yes, grandson, and then on top of all that, the Williams family built a second building on Greenwood Avenue in 1914. And in that building, there was the huge Williams Dreamland Theater that could seat 700 people! It featured movies and live musicals. The building also had a 21-room boarding house. In 1914, a Black Oklahoma newspaper, Black Dispatch, named Mrs. Loula Williams Oklahoma's best Black businesswoman. Loula Williams also owned theaters in Okmulgee and Muskogee," Grandme said.

The Black DISPATCH
FAITH

Mrs. Loula Williams Oklahoma's best Black businesswoman. Loula Williams also owns theaters in Okmulgee and Muskogee.

WILLIAM'S DREAMLAND THEATRE WILLIAM'S THEATER THEATRE

WILLIAMS DREAMLAND THEATER

Oklahoma Sun

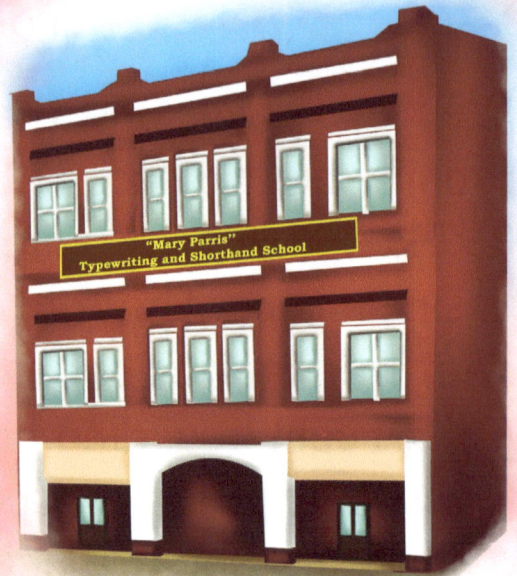

"Mary Parris"
Typewriting and Shorthand School

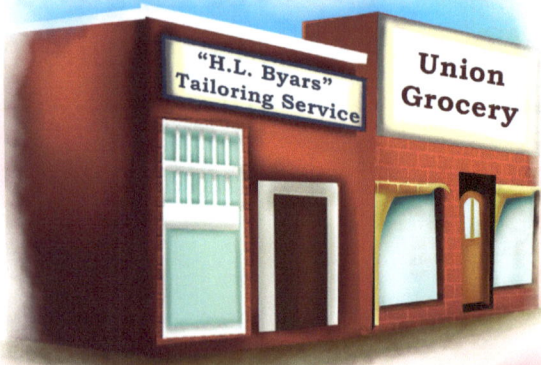

"H.L. Byars"
Tailoring Service

Union
Grocery

"Grandme, what other businesses did they have in the Greenwood District?" asked Keith.

Grandme wasted no time listing more businesses. "J. T. Taylor and J. L. Duncan owned Union Grocery on Greenwood Avenue, The Oklahoma Sun newspaper was at 101 ½ North Greenwood, Mary Parris' typewriting and shorthand school was at 103 ½ North Greenwood Avenue, and H. L. Byars had a tailor business at 105 North Greenwood Avenue."

Grandme was now on a roll. "There was also O. W. Gurley, who owned Gurley Hotel, at 112 North Greenwood. Oh, let me tell you about Mr. Gurley. He was a highly intelligent educator and entrepreneur who made tons of money buying and selling land. He purchased 40 acres in Tulsa and sold it only to Black people. Mr. Gurley's property lines included Pine Street, Frisco railroad tracks, Lansing Avenue, and Cincinnati Ave."

Keith was just as impressed as Grandme. "I have been on all of those streets. That's HUGE!"

"You are exactly right, grandson. It was HUGE," exclaimed Grandme. "Mr. Gurley's first business was a rooming house, and then he built three two-story buildings and five residences. On top of all that, he bought an 80-acre farm in Rogers County."

"Really, Grandme?" asked Keith.

"Yes, sir, and he also founded what today is called Vernon AME Church," explained Grandme.

"Wow! Mr. Gurley was a true entrepreneur. I want to be like that when I grow up," said Keith.

"Grandson, I believe you have that entrepreneurial intelligence," replied Grandme.

N Greenwood 119

N Greenwood 202

RED WING
DRUG STORE

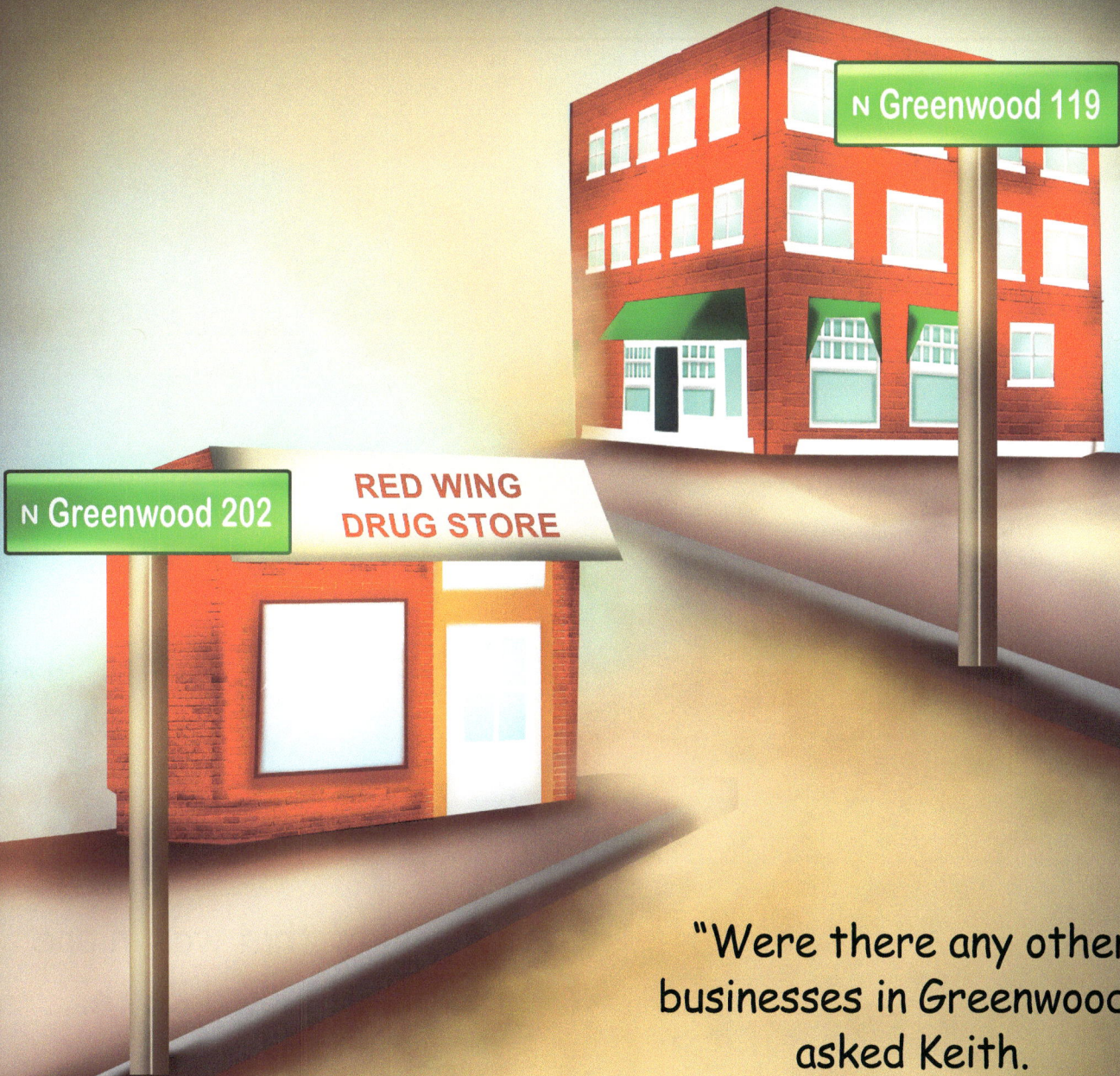

"Were there any other
businesses in Greenwood?"
asked Keith.

"Yes, sir, there sure were," explained Grandme.
"Mr. Anderson owned the Y. M. C. A. Tailors at 114
North Greenwood Avenue, and at 119 North Greenwood
there was a two-story building that housed Carter's
Barbershop, a pool hall, meeting rooms, and a cigar
store. There was also a pharmacy W. M. Kyle owned at
202 North Greenwood named the Red Wing Drug Store."

"Wow, all of that was in one building?" asked Keith.

"Yes, grandson, it sure was! Plus, Mrs. M. N. Hardy owned a Madam C. J. Walker Beauty Parlor at 210 North Greenwood Avenue."

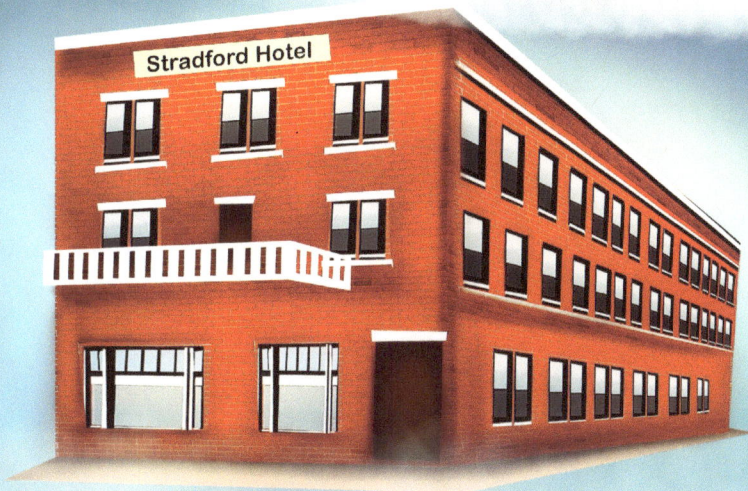

"Grandson, Mr. J. B. Stradford's hotel at 301 North Greenwood was the largest African American-owned hotel in the United States. In the extravagant Stradford Hotel, Black people enjoyed all the amenities of the downtown hotels that served Whites only. The hotel had state-of-the-art suites, a formal restaurant, and a café. Mr. Stradford owned a real estate and a loan and investment business in the same hotel," Grandme explained.

"The Tulsa Star was at 501 North Greenwood Avenue. A. J. Smitherman was its owner and editor. This was the first daily Black newspaper with national distribution, and it was a useful resource for Black people to stay notified about topics involving them throughout the U.S., said Grandme.

"Grandme, did Black people have any other businesses outside Greenwood Avenue?" asked Keith.

"Yes, grandson, we sure did! That's why it's called the Greenwood District, because Blacks owned several businesses and homes on different streets," Grandme explained. "North Elgin Grocery and Confectionary was at 404 North Elgin Street."

"What's a confectionary?" Keith asked.

Grandme answered, "It's another word for candy store."

"Oh, that sounds like that would have been my favorite place," Keith said.

Grandme continued with her story. "Mr. J. L. Grier owned a shoe shop at 518 East Archer Street, and Mrs. Dora Wells owned a women's clothing store called Wells Garment Factory at 613 East Archer Street. Then there was the Jackson Undertaking Company at 622 East Archer, and Mr. and Mrs. Cornelius Hunter owned the Liberty Café at 16 North Cincinnati Avenue."

"Pharmacist Mr. P. S. Thompson owned The Druggist at 23 North Cincinnati and if you wanted a Coca-Cola, you could buy it at Rolly and Ada Huff's Confectionary on Archer between Detroit and Cincinnati," said Grandme.

"Mabel Little owned the Little Rose Beauty Salon at 615 East Indiana Avenue. Her business specialized in hair styling, facials, and manicures. She also owned a restaurant next to her salon and owned rental properties with her husband," said Grandme.

"Grandme, that's a lot of businesses, but were there any parks in the neighborhood?" asked Keith.

"Yes, sir! I'm so glad you asked," said Grandme. "With the profits from Mr. Simon Berry's various businesses, he reinvested in the Black community by purchasing land and establishing a park which included a dance hall and picnic areas. It was the first park with a swimming pool and recreation facilities in North Tulsa. Today it is known as Lincoln Park."

"Grandme, these businesses sound amazing! But Mom and I drove down Greenwood Avenue last week, and I don't remember seeing any of them, so are you sure all this really happened?" Keith asked.

"Yes, grandson, every bit of this story is true! But unfortunately, this story doesn't have a happy ending. The entire Greenwood District, including its businesses and homes, was bombed, burned, and reduced to ashes during what was later called the Tulsa Race Massacre on May 31 and June 1, 1921. Actually, the first bombs that ever fell on American soil were on Black Wall Street, right here in Tulsa, Oklahoma," Grandme said with tears in her eyes.

"I have never heard of that. What happened, Grandme? And why? This is too horrible to even think of," Keith said, looking shocked.

"I know it's horrific and really unbelievable, but it is true. Unfortunately, the cause of these events boils down to jealousy, racism, and hatred," explained Grandme.

Keith asked, "What is racism?"

"Racism is the unfair treatment of people based on their skin color," Grandme responded.

"What does racism have to do with all the businesses and homes being burned down?" Keith asked.

"Some believe White residents burned them down because they were racist and considered Blacks inferior to them because of their skin color. They didn't want them to enjoy the success of their thriving community. Others say the massacre took place because of a misunderstanding in an elevator. But I will address that later in the story," Grandme explained.

"These horrific events started when White residents, including the police, sheriffs, and the National Guard ambushed the Black community in the Greenwood District and destroyed 600 businesses, 21 churches, 21 restaurants, 30 grocery stores, two movie theaters, six private planes, a hospital, a bank, post office, schools, and libraries," Grandme said.

"Now, grandson, this is where this story gets pretty heartbreaking," said Grandme. "On May 31, most of Booker T. Washington's high school students were preparing for prom and graduation. They were so excited. It was the social event of the school year. The students and faculty had decorated the school and streets surrounding it."

Booker T. Washington's high school

"Grandme, that sounds fun and exciting; there's nothing heartbreaking about that," said Keith.

"Yes, grandson, but events soon turned tragic. An adult entered the school and told the students to go home immediately and prepare for danger," Grandme explained.

"Why would he do that?" Keith asked.

"He had just read a shocking newspaper headline in the Tulsa Tribune, 'To Lynch Negro Tonight.' Others say the headline read, 'Nab Negro for Attacking Girl in Elevator.' No one knows exactly what it said because the surviving copies were changed," Grandme replied.

The Tulsa Tribune

"To Lynch Negro Tonight."

"Grandme, what happened?" asked Keith.

Grandme responded, "The day before, on May 30, a 17-year-old White girl Sarah Page accused a 19-year-old Black boy Dick Rowland of criminally assaulting her in an elevator in the Drexel Building. Sarah later said she made the whole thing up and Mr. Rowland never assaulted her. However, the damage was already done."

"Grandme, what do you mean 'the damage was already done?'" asked Keith.

"Unfortunately, the police picked up Mr. Rowland the very next day, questioned him, and put him in jail. In Sarah's statement to police, she admitted her encounter with Mr. Rowland had been totally innocent, that he had come close to her in the elevator, and accidentally stepped on her foot. But she also explained how she'd overreacted, panicked, and slapped Rowland, and he'd grabbed her arm to prevent her from slapping him again. She'd screamed, and he'd run, fearing for his life," explained Grandme.

"OK, Grandme, did they let him out of jail when she said he didn't do it? And did she get in trouble for not being truthful in the first place?" asked Keith.

"She did not get into trouble, but unfortunately, Rowland and the Black community weren't so lucky," Grandme explained. "News of the so-called 'assault' spread like wildfire, thanks primarily to the White newspaper reports. Later that day, the Greenwood District heard rumors that 400 White men had surrounded Rowland's jail and planned to lynch him. So, about 30 armed Black men emerged from the Greenwood District and went to the jail to protect Rowland, however, the sheriff and police convinced them to go home."

"Later that evening, another rumor circulated throughout the Greenwood District that White men had stormed the jail where Rowland was located, and the crowd had grown to approximately 2000 people, so 75 Black men returned to the jail. A White Sheriff named McCulloch, and a Black officer named Barney Cleaver persuaded the Black men to leave again. However, when a White man tried to take away a Black man's gun, a shot rang out during the struggle, and in a split second the situation went from bad to worse," Grandme said.

"Grandme, what happened next?" asked Keith.

"White residents, the Tulsa Police Department, the Tulsa Sheriff's Department, and the National Guard led an inhumane attack on Greenwood District's residents over a two-day period. First, the Whites surrounded the Greenwood District with 60 to 80 cars, rifles, pistols, machine guns, and bombs. Then, they entered the district and systematically captured African Americans while looting and burning their buildings and homes. They also used planes in the massacre. As fighting became more intense, White residents also set fire to buildings in and around the Frisco Railroad Depot," Grandme explained.

"The White men looted Black-owned hardware, pawn, and sports shops to steal their guns. They took over $43,000 worth of ammunition and anything else they could get their hands on," Grandme said.

"They shot locks off doors, snatched photographs and telephones off the walls, set flammable items on fire, and stole silverware and jewelry. White boys as young as 10 years old participated in the mayhem and horror," Grandme said with disapproval.

"The Tulsa Police Force learned of the crisis and received orders to stop Black men from entering the White district by any means necessary. They took the Black residents captured during the fighting to jail, leaving the Greenwood District defenseless against the White residents of Tulsa," said Grandme.

"White men volunteered to help the police and even offered their personal vehicles for assistance. The police deputized and gave special permission to over 500 White volunteers to help them unlawfully fight the Black residents in the Greenwood District. The Tulsa Chief of Police also requested the help of the National Guard when they felt they could not handle the situation," Grandme stated.

"Grandme, all of this is just horrible! What happened to the families with children, and the older people that couldn't defend themselves?" Keith asked.

"Yes, grandson, words can't describe the horror!" Grandme explained. "Well, on top of all that, there was no mercy for elderly people. An elderly Black couple was shot in the back of their heads while they prayed! Then the perpetrators robbed them of their valuables and set their house on fire."

"Grandme, was there anywhere Black people could go to hide from the violence?" asked Keith.

"Armed guards took popular Black surgeon, Dr. Andrew C. Jackson, to Convention Hall for his protection, but a White teenager shot and killed him before he reached his destination. The Convention Hall on 105 East Brady Street was one of the main detention centers. Fifteen hundred Black residents were detained there under armed guard. McNulty Park, between Detroit and Elgin avenues, was also a detention center that held over 4,000 Black people," Grandme said.

"Grandme, what about the churches? Could Black people hide in churches?" asked Keith.

"Grandson, they tried. Over 50 Black people barricaded themselves into a church. The White residents tried to pry their way into the church, however they could not get in, so they just set the entire church on fire! Twenty-one churches, including Mt. Zion Baptist church, were reduced to ashes," Grandme replied.

"Grandme, this is too horrendous to be true!" exclaimed Keith.

"I know, grandson, it's hard to believe. On June 2, the day after the massacre, about 10,000 Black people were homeless because their homes had been destroyed. The Red Cross provided them with clothing, water, and food. The Black hospital was burned to rubble, leaving nowhere for injured Blacks to seek medical attention. Some public buildings, schools, and churches outside the Greenwood District helped with accommodation," said Grandme.

"Horribly, grandson, a lot of Black people died during this massacre. Although reports indicate 300 people died, some say up to 3,000 were buried in mass graves. Property damage was more than $1.5 million in commercial real estate and $750,000 in personal property. In today's money, it would be more," said Grandme.

"Grandme, why didn't the police help them?" asked Keith, looking disappointed.

"Well, some police helped," explained Grandme. "However, an investigation later found that special officers in the police were ringleaders in the killings. Tulsa police chief, John Gustafson, was later found guilty of conspiracy and neglect for his actions on June 30, 1921."

"Grandme, what happened to Dick Rowland and Sarah Page?" asked Keith.

"Dick Rowland was found not guilty, and rumor has it Rowland and Page fled the state and moved to Kansas City together," said Grandme.

"Grandme, hopefully they had a happy ending, but it's hard to imagine that was the case in Tulsa with so many lives and businesses lost," said Keith.

"Grandson, unfortunately, there is no happy ending. And it's not over yet. A group of Oklahomans filed a lawsuit for reparations, which the U.S. Supreme court rejected in 2005. However, a case was reopened in 2020 on the grounds of the massacre continuing to be a public nuisance. It is widely believed Tulsa officials are 'enriching themselves by promoting the site of the massacre as a tourist attraction,' although the people of the Greenwood District have received no substantial benefit from those endeavors."

"The complainants asked the City of Tulsa and other local government entities for reparations for the ongoing devastation the race massacre caused.

This includes the three surviving Oklahomans from the Tulsa Race Massacre: Hughes Van Ellis, Mother Lessie Benningfield Randle, and Viola Fletcher who still suffers from emotional and physical distress from these events," Grandme said.

"Grandme, what are reparations?" Keith asked.

Grandme responded, "Reparations are money given for abuse or injury, but in this case, it seems to be much more than that. People's lives and businesses were destroyed and even now, 100 years later, the Tulsa Massacre still affects the Black residents of Tulsa today. Our city is still divided. Many Black people still live in North Tulsa with few resources. Black Wall Street has never been the same since those events."

"Wow, Grandme!" Keith exclaimed. "This was not the story time I was expecting! Although I was ready to play my video game, you have taught me so much. I have never heard of the successes of Black Wall Street before or about its destruction."

"I feel very sad about all the businesses and lives lost, but I also feel a sense of pride. I am proud to learn about all the businesses Black people created and how they worked together and supported one another. It has inspired me to become a business owner and an entrepreneur."

"Maybe I can help rebuild Black Wall Street to what it once was. Perhaps it might yet become the promise land. I like the sound of a movie theater with video gaming centers and Beyblade tournaments. If we rebuilt all the amenities of Black Wall Street, it would no longer be just a memory lane to wander down. I can't wait to have another story time with you, but are you ready to play this video game with me now?" asked Keith.

"Yes, Keith, I'm ready to try your video game. I might even beat you!" said Grandme.

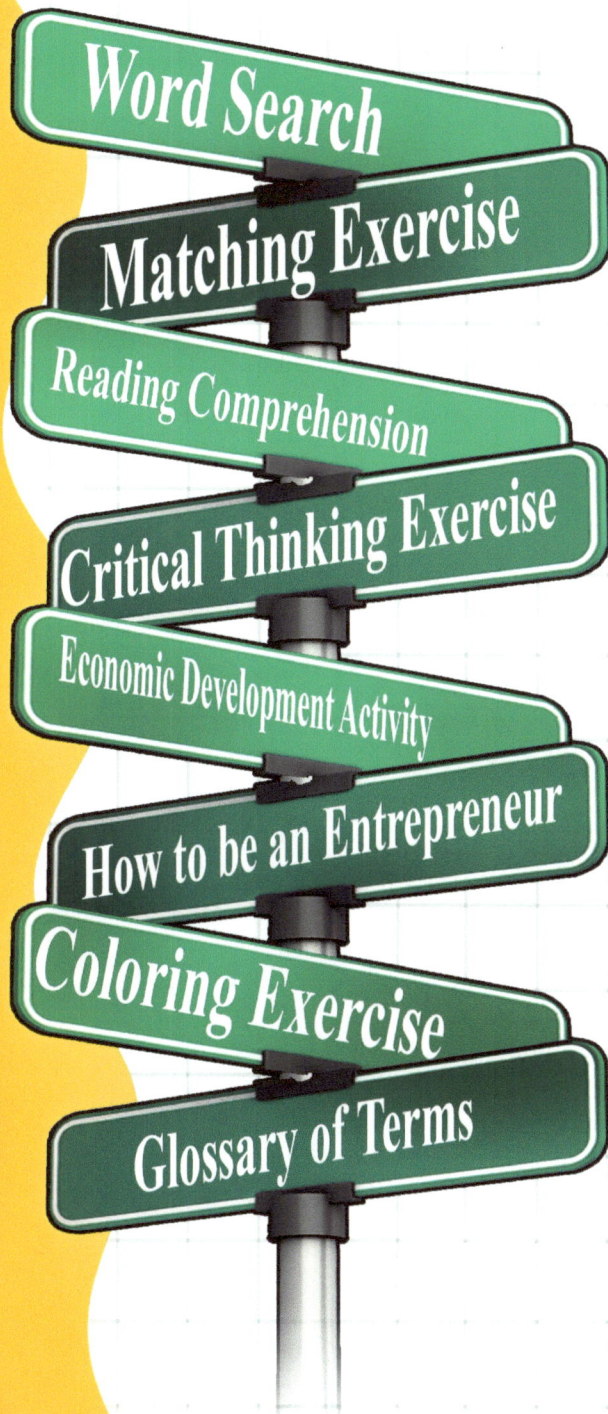

Activities

Word Search

Matching Exercise

Reading Comprehension

Critical Thinking Exercise

Economic Development Activity

How to be an Entrepreneur

Coloring Exercise

Glossary of Terms

- Word Search
- Matching Exercise
- Reading Comprehension
- Critical Thinking Exercise
- Economic Development Activity
- How to be an Entrepreneur
- Coloring Exercise
- Glossary of Terms

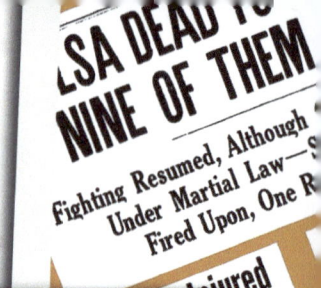

A Promised Deferred: The Massacre of Black Wall Street
Word Search

```
S B P O E Y T T L P D F S F L B R T F J
P E C I V I L A A V O H M V L G A V G M
R L G L M X N G I Q O Y M A D I C K A B
O R D R T D E M R C W N C J H U E S Z U
M R L R E E V O C X N K Q I C L S W R T
I R O W O G E C R Y E L R U G A E U A U
S R E W B F A R R S E E N K C L E K A R
E E W H L F D T T F R Z Z R D N E O Y B
D H A Z C A O A I S G H E N E A L O I V
G T S B G T N P R O L I A R T S V S A U
C O L W T J E D B T N R P S L R N C U R
K M U B P H W L Y V S E P A A A L R I C
L F T G L D B N F Q R X L R I E V M G J
J U M R Z T Y F G T P S H A K T M A X Q
N B A P Y I P E N N Q E J H M I H H C D
G T O M R X U E I Y T M I D J I Z A K V
S L Z Y U E D L P J K Q L W T P R X Z J
H N G V P L S C R O W Y W C L L A W M D
X X D U U Q Z C P Q Y D C Y W V G Y U X
J K O H F J N V K V H B K X E Q Q D M O
```

Black Wall Street	Promised Land
Greenwood	O. W. Gurley
Jim Crow	J. B. Stradford
Segregation	Tulsa Star
Race Massacre	Dick Rowland
Trail of Tears	Sarah Page
Entrepreneur	Viola Fletcher
Civil War	Mother Randle

Matching Exercise
Match the words in the left-hand column with the correct definition on the right.

Bias	To give someone the power to enforce the law
Deputize	A violent public disturbance that law enforcement cannot control
Discrimination	A strong feeling or opinion, positive or negative, with no information to justify it
Entrepreneur	The successful African American business district in Tulsa
Greenwood District	Preconceived opinion not based on reason or experience
	A person that starts and runs a business
Jim Crow laws	The killing of a person by a group without a legal trial
Looting	Laws that promoted segregation and racist practices
Lynching	Deliberately and violently killing many people
Massacre	Deciding one group is better or worse than other groups and acting on that belief. Those actions can include the exclusion of that group from activities, locations, etc.
Prejudice	
Riot	Mass stealing from homes and businesses, especially during periods of unrest

Reading Comprehension

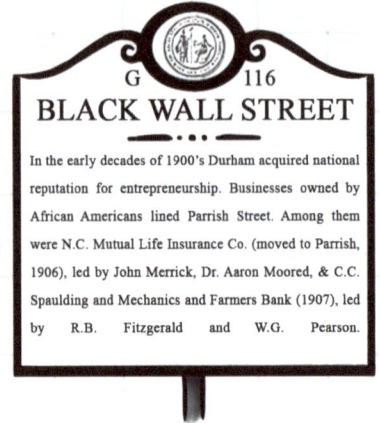

Jim Crow laws existed in the United States in the late 19th and early 20th century to enforce segregation between Black and White people in public places such as restrooms, schools, and transportation. Black Americans could not shop at the same places as White Americans. Jim Crow laws also made it difficult for Black people to vote. Although the laws were disheartening, Black Oklahomans turned a negative situation into a positive one and created a thriving community called Black Wall Street in Tulsa. Black Wall Street had over 600 businesses including grocery stores, restaurants, movie theaters, churches, a bank, a post office, schools, and libraries. Tragically, in 1920 a White racist mob destroyed all the businesses there, massacred well over 300 Black people, detained 4,000 in detention centers, and left over 10,000 homeless. This catastrophe in American history is called the Tulsa Race Massacre.

Visualize
Text to Mind

Critical Thinking

Jim Crow and Segregation

RESTROOMS
WHITE   COLORED

WHITES   COLORED

There is a long history of segregation in the United States of America and Tulsa, Oklahoma is not any different. This is thanks to Jim Crow laws enacted in the late 19th and early 20th centuries, including the Racial Segregation Ordinance of 1916 that made it unlawful for White and Black people to live, eat, and shop together. The Jim Crow laws were overturned by the Civil Rights Act of 1964 and the Voting Rights Act of 1965.

Read the Racial Segregation Ordinance for Tulsa, Oklahoma below.

> BE IT ORDAINED BY THE BOARD OF COMMISSIONERS
> OF THE CITY OF TULSA, OKLAHOMA:
>
> SECTION 1. It shall be unlawful for any white person to move into and occupy as a residence or place of abode any house in any block situated within the City of Tulsa, Oklahoma, upon which 75 per cent of the residents occupying said block are colored people. It shall be unlawful for any white person to establish and maintain a hotel, rooming house or place of public assembly upon any block in said city upon which 75 per cent or more of the residents, roomers, guests, or boarders in such block are colored persons.
>
> SECTION 2. It shall be unlawful for any colored person to move into and occupy as a residence or place of abode, any house in any block situated within the City of Tulsa, Oklahoma, upon which 75 per cent of the residents occupying said block are white people. It shall be unlawful for any colored person to establish and maintain a hotel, rooming house, or place of public assembly upon any block in said city upon which 75 per cent or more of the residents, roomers, guests, or boarders in such block, are white persons.

How did the Racial Segregation Ordinance help the Greenwood District prosper?

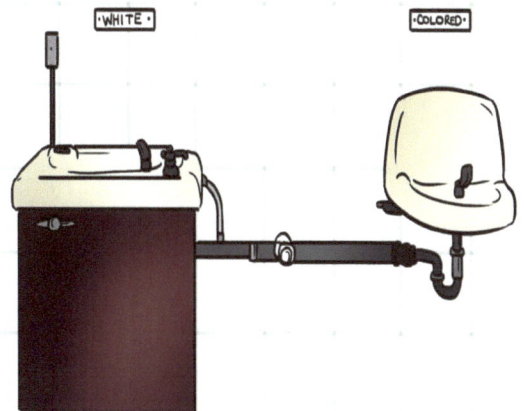

· WHITE ·   · COLORED ·

_____

_____

_____

_____

_____

_____

_____

Economic Development Exercise
Build a Community

Economic development is crucial in building community. Tulsa's segregation laws forced the Greenwood District to become self-sufficient, but it also meant all the money made in Greenwood stayed in the district. Thanks to several highly intelligent and creative African American entrepreneurs, over 600 businesses were created in Tulsa to meet the needs of its residents. Below is a list of 14 institutions and businesses that existed in the Greenwood District in 1920. Next to the business name, choose a category from the list above. Some can be used more than once.

Education	Entertainment	Retail	Hospitality	Services
Healthcare	Religion	Press	Transportation	

1. Williams Dreamland Theatre _____

2. Union Grocery _____

3. The Oklahoma Sun newspaper _____

4. Gurley Hotel _____

5. Vernon AME Church _____

6. Y. M. C. A Tailors _____

7. Carter's Barbershop _____

8. Red Wing Drug Store (Pharmacy) _____

9. Madam C. J. Walker Beauty Parlor _____

10. Stradford Hotel _____

11. Tulsa Star newspaper _____

12. Wells Garment Factory _____

13. Nickel-a-Ride Car Service _____

14. Booker T. Washington High School _____

How to be an Entrepreneur

According to the book, How to Turn $100 into $1,000,000, a great business idea must be different, desirable, and dynamic. This is what the African American entrepreneurs of the Greenwood District did because of the segregation laws that tried to hold them back. See if you can come up with a great business idea too! Complete the chart below.

Consider	Example answer	Example of a money-making idea	Your answer	Your money-making idea
Something you love doing	Playing video games	Create video game tutorials		
Something you are great at	Math	Become a math tutor		
Something you appreciate	Family	Make family picture books		
Something people don't have but need	T-shirts for their cause	Create them		
Whom do you look up to, and what does that person do?	My mother who writes books	Write a book		

Coloring Exercise

Color in the picture below that celebrates the entrepreneurs and residents of Black Wall Street.

Glossary of Terms

Bias: A strong feeling or opinion, positive or negative, with no information to justify it

Deputize: To give someone the power to enforce the law

Discrimination: Deciding one group is better or worse than other groups and acting on that belief

Entrepreneur: A person who starts and runs a business

Greenwood District: The successful African American business district in Tulsa, Oklahoma

Jim Crow laws: Laws that promoted segregation and racist practices

Loot: Massive stealing from homes and businesses, especially during periods of unrest

Lynching: The killing of a person by a group without a legal trial

Massacre: Deliberately and violently killing many people

Prejudice: A preconceived opinion not based on reason or experience

Racism: The unfair treatment of people based on their skin color

Reparations: Money given for abuse or injury

Riot: A violent public disturbance that law enforcement can not control

Segregation: Systemic separation in a society or country to set someone or something apart in daily life. In racial segregation, like under Jim Crow laws, there is separation of people into racial or other ethnic groups.

Economic Development Exercise
Build a Community

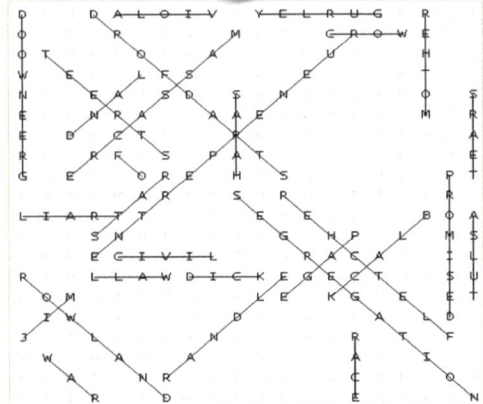

1. Entertainment
2. Retail
3. Press
4. Hospitality
5. Religion
6. Services
7. Services
8. Healthcare
9. Services
10. Hospitality
11. Press
12. Retail
13. Transportation
14. Education

Word Search

Matching Exercise

Bias	To give someone the power to enforce the law
Deputize	A violent public disturbance that law enforcement cannot control
Discrimination	A strong feeling or opinion, positive or negative, with no information to justify it
Entrepreneur	The successful African American business district in Tulsa
Greenwood District	Preconceived opinion not based on reason or experience
Jim Crow laws	A person that starts and runs a business
Looting	The killing of a person by a group without a legal trial
Lynching	Laws that promoted segregation and racist practices
Massacre	Deliberately and violently killing many people
Prejudice	Deciding one group is better or worse than other groups and acting on that belief. Those actions can include the exclusion of that group from activities, locations, etc.
Riot	Mass stealing from homes and businesses, especially during periods of unrest